ROOM AND TIME ENOUGH

ROOM AND TIME ENOUGH

The Land of Mary Austin

Photographs by Morley Baer

Introduction by Augusta Fink   Lines by Mary Austin

 NORTHLAND PRESS • FLAGSTAFF, ARIZONA • 1979

frontispiece: Enchanted Mesa, near Ácoma

Selections from Mary Austin's *The Lands of the Sun*
(Boston: Houghton Mifflin Company, 1927) have been
reprinted by permission of the School of American
Research, Santa Fe, New Mexico.

CONTENTS

PROLOGUE

FOR A PHOTOGRAPHER, to read Mary Austin is to invite an intense and enveloping challenge. Her pen all but demands visual accompaniment. The vast scale of her interests in the West are found in its magnificences as well as in its minutiae. Her legacy, however, lies not only in the land but in her preoccupation with its spirit and with how this force re-energizes and fortifies man.

Her writing has always been a beneficent merger: a recognition of those great natural strengths in open space of land, sea, and air is interwoven with distinctly feminine accents derived from an imperturbably direct curiosity. She speaks of the ordinary in land and man and, by so speaking, gives them extraordinary meanings.

My affinity with the lands that Mary Austin writes about started almost a lifetime ago when my grandfather returned to Ohio almost every summer from a trip to the West Coast. For months he would hold me transfixed with stories of the distant country he had seen. At school or at play, I would often stand apart, still distracted by what I had listened to the night before. I imagined vast desert flats with a sparse plant or two, heroic granite peaks on every mountaintop, a long stretching shoreline running south forever, and a lonely ranch set against the foothills with one white horse in the corral.

Does one ever forget such dreams? Years later, when they were revived and enhanced by Mary Austin's simple, direct stories, the combination produced a motive and an energy that no youngster in Ohio could have counted on.

It was in Mary Austin's writing that I first discovered the identification of person and place and how each reinforces the other. I had never been to the land of lost borders or looked at the sierra from the land of little rain. But I was close. I now began to know them, to believe in them, and to feel their import in an imagery so incessant, so compelling that again I was transported, this time with a precipitous force to go there to photograph. The land was there! I was almost in it! To take one more step was to see joyously, to feel intensely, to photograph with sheer impulse, and to become part of the *place*.

In the immensity of California and the Southwest, Mary Austin's word is like a mothering power, a gently aggressive gathering of those attitudes that help me to understand the land in which I live.

MORLEY BAER
Carmel, California

INTRODUCTION

WRITER, MYSTIC, WOMAN, Mary Austin lived ahead of her times and in a sense outside of all time. Of her, Carl Van Doren wrote, "Her books were wells driven into America to bring up water for her countrymen though they might not have realized their thirst."

Author of some thirty books and more than 250 articles and other short pieces, she was among the foremost writers of the early part of this century. Her writing ranged in subject matter from anthropology and folklore to metaphysics and the arts. It took every literary form from novel to nature essay. But it reached its most memorable levels of expression when she wrote of the earth, illuminating not only the landscape but the spirit of the West.

Mary Austin's country is a land of light and air, of limitless space and sky, of great granite mountains and gleaming desert sand, of forsaken mesas and sea-breasting hills. It was in the vast "Country of Lost Borders," beneath the towering thrust of the Sierra Nevada, that her love affair with the land began. And it was amidst the windswept mesas and majestic mountains of New Mexico that she ended her days. Through the lens of her highly personalized and imagistic style, it is possible to perceive the quality of this country: awesome in its immensity, yet intimate in its compelling hold upon the affections.

Mary Hunter Austin was twenty before she came to dwell in her heartland. Born in the small midwestern community of Carlinville, Illinois, on September 9, 1868, she was a descendant of pioneer settlers not unfamiliar with the hardships of a frontier existence. Raised in the ambience of a matriarchal society, she absorbed the proud precepts of her maternal forebears and learned to emulate their examples of intrepid womanhood. But it was from her father, whom she adored, that she received her initiation into the never-ending enchantment of books and the myriad wonders of the outdoors.

George Hunter was a scholarly man whose health had been impaired during his service as a captain in the Civil War. Prevented by chronic illness from aggressively pursuing his profession as an attorney, he could provide only a meager income for his family. His wife, Susanna, harassed by financial problems and troubled by the incipient lameness of their two-year-old son, James, had bitterly resented the advent of Mary's birth.

From her earliest years, Mary was aware that her mother disliked her. The fact that she was a precocious and nonconforming child, with strange flashes of intuition and an overly active imagination, augmented the estrangement. Baffled and hurt, the lonely little girl yearned for the mother's love denied her. Then, before she was six, two powerful, ontological experiences brought her the security that would be a refuge for the rest of her life.

The first of these was the discovery of an invulnerable Self, whom she henceforth referred to as "I-Mary": the alter ego who was entirely self-sufficient and had no need to be accepted or loved. Not long afterward, on a hilltop near her home, she experienced a transcendent encounter with her natural surroundings that transformed her perception of reality to an expanded level of consciousness. Out of these experiences came the foundation for both her mysticism and the acute sensitivity to nature that was to imbue her finest writings.

Despite her preoccupation with ideas beyond her years, Mary's childhood was not unhappy. Through her talent for inventing spine-tingling tales of adventure, she attracted a coterie of devoted playmates, and with her younger sister, Jennie, she shared a close and satisfying relationship. Best of all were the hours she spent with her father, whether on long walks in the countryside or in his well-stocked library. There her passion for books was nurtured. By the time she was seven, she had announced her intention to become a writer and begun to experiment with putting words together to record simple plots.

Then, in her tenth year, Mary's snug little world fell apart. Within less than two months, both her father and her beloved Jennie were dead: the latter of diphtheria and the former of a mysterious ailment that could have been cancer.

A deeply troubled adolescence ensued. The loss of the two people who had been most precious to her left her desolate. Even her ability to find comfort in communion with nature, or within the security of her inner self, temporarily deserted her. Only her enthusiasm for books and her determination to write remained constant.

As she grew into young womanhood, the tendencies toward willfulness and nonconformity that she had demonstrated as a child became more pronounced. She refused to accept conventional patterns of behavior or to subordinate her ideas and opinions in order to gain approval. This resulted in an unpopularity with the opposite sex that even her fierce independence could not completely ignore. Withdrawn and aloof, she hid her sensitivity to rejection behind a screen of haughty detachment, which only served to worsen the situation.

Psychosomatic illnesses began to plague her. Twice during her college years, she was forced to abandon her classes. But in June 1888 she graduated from Blackburn College, having majored in science and reluctantly prepared to teach. At this point, Susanna Hunter decided to take Mary and her twelve-year-old brother George to California, where Susanna's elder son, Jim, had filed a homestead claim on land near Bakersfield, in the southern end of the San Joaquin Valley. Mary went along without much protest, confident that she could write in one place as well as another. Unaware of the fateful encounter with the land that awaited her, she embarked on the journey that would determine the course of her career.

Almost immediately upon her arrival in California, Mary became avidly interested in her environment. The country spoke to her with a strange insistence that compelled an equally intense response. Her new home was a one-room cabin set in the midst of sagebrush, encircled on three sides by mountains. There she slept little and spent most of her time outdoors, eagerly studying the habits of wildlife and the unfamiliar aspect of native plants. Often she sat for hours in the moonlight to watch the frisking of field mice or the mating of elf owls. Early in the morning she was out again, sometimes following a bobcat to its lair and crouching before its den, without fear, to contemplate the wild creature.

Adjacent to the family homestead was the 100,000-acre Rancho El Tejon, owned by General Edward Fitzgerald Beale. An early pioneer, Beale possessed a prodigious knowledge about California and the West. Fortunately for Mary, he became her friend. Patiently, in long talks, he satisfied her thirst for information about the history, geography, and folklore of the Tejon country. In addition, he let her roam at will through his huge acreage, instructing his *majordomos* to pave the way for her contacts with the Indians, sheepherders, and *vaqueros* who lived there. She attended roundups, brandings, and *bailes*. She also learned about the care of the flock, the procedures for clipping wool, and the festivities that followed the shearings. What Mary saw and heard, she recorded in a ten-cent notebook, which later would provide the raw material for her writing. Portions of five books were to stem in part from her experiences in the San Joaquin Valley: *The Land of Little Rain*, *Isidro*, *The Flock*, *Lost Borders*, and *The Ford*.

General Beale's interest in Mary extended to the problems of her family. When a severe drought destroyed their hope of a thriving farm, he offered them occupancy of a stage hostelry near their homestead and arranged for them to run it as a roadside inn. The venture was successful but required hard work, to which Mary's contribution was small. Chagrined, she resolved to become financially independent and, in 1889, obtained a teaching position in the Kern County Schools, about ten miles from Bakersfield. There she boarded with a congenial family and met the man who was to be her husband.

Stafford Wallace Austin was a quiet, scholarly man, seven years Mary's senior. Son of a prominent Hawaii family, he was well educated and possessed all the qualities of a gentleman. Moreover, Mary saw him as her intellectual equal. Her encounters with other young men had not been rewarding. Thin and pale, with only her abundant, reddish brown hair as a claim to beauty, she alienated local youths by her blunt manner and unwillingness to play up to their egos. But Wallace Austin seemed to appreciate her for her real self.

Their courtship proceeded through the spring and summer of 1890, and on May 19, 1891, they were married. Wallace's wedding present to Mary was a gold, pearl-handled pen, which she took as a sign that he sympathized with her ambition to be a writer. They settled in a small house on the twenty-acre fruit farm Austin was trying to cultivate. Untrained for the enterprise, he was soon faced with failure. After drifting from one odd job to another, he grasped the opportunity to join his brother in a land reclamation project located in the Owens Valley.

While Mary was briefly left alone to pack their belongings, she wrote her first two short stories. They were simple tales based on material she had gathered in the Tejon country. The one entitled "The Mother of Felipe" captured the harsh beauty of the land in a style that would be the hallmark of her later nature writing. And in both stories, the vivid characterizations and rhythmic prose gave promise of the artistry she was to develop. With no difficulty, she sold them to *The Overland Monthly*, a San Francisco magazine.

The Owens Valley, in which Mary was to live for fourteen years, was high desert country that lay between the towering Sierra Nevada Range to the west and the massive Inyo Mountains to the east. It was an isolated, lonely land, inhabited by sheepherders, miners, and Paiute Indians. It was also a land of overwhelming splendor that at first sight struck upon Mary's senses with a resounding chord.

The Austins found lodging in the tiny town of Lone Pine, renting a room in its one hotel. There Mary, who was six-months pregnant, sat on the porch, gazing at the awesome grandeur of soaring mountain peaks, or strolled through the dusty lanes of the Mexican quarter, where she easily related to the conviviality of the buxom *señoras*. Then, suddenly, the serenity of her existence was shattered. Wallace lost his job, and the Austins were evicted for not paying their rent. To support herself, as well as her impecunious spouse, Mary took a job as a cook in a nearby boardinghouse, where she stayed through the summer.

In September she sought shelter in her mother's home in Bakersfield for the birth of her baby. It proved an excruciatingly difficult delivery, and it is possible that the daughter, born on October 30, 1892, may have sustained brain damage during the ordeal. Mary did learn, however, some years later, that there were recessive traits on both sides of Wallace's family. Whatever the cause, it soon become evident that the child, named Ruth, was mentally retarded. It was a heartbreaking discovery that brought Mary years of anguish.

In order to earn money for Ruth's medical care, Mary taught school, first in Bishop and then in Lone Pine, where Wallace was for a time superintendent of the Inyo County Schools. Meanwhile, she forged lasting friendships with the Indians who dwelt in campoodies close by, sharing in their activities and taking particular pleasure in witnessing their religious ceremonies. It was the beginning of her advocacy of Indian rights, which later developed into a lifelong crusade. It was also the means by which she garnered material for several of her books, including *The American Rhythm*, *The Basket Woman*, and two of the essays in *The Land of Little Rain*. But the most dramatic result of her association with the aborigines was a giant leap in her evolution as a mystic.

From medicine men at the Bishop campoody, she learned about the Paiute practice of prayer. They believed in a creative force, accessible to man and responsive to any emergency, whether it be sickness or the need for rain. Through sustained rhythmic movement and sound, such as their ceremonial chants and dances, they placed themselves in harmony with the universal principle of all creation and brought their desires to pass. Freedom from distraction and detachment from habitual modes of thinking were prerequisites for success.

These concepts were in accord with Mary's mystical inclinations and, in addition, offered a practical application to everyday problems. Experimenting with this approach to prayer, she found an increased ability to concentrate, which sharpened her writing skills. Then a chance encounter with the philosopher William James confirmed her emerging conviction that the secret of creativity was in that area of the mind usually referred to as the subconscious. Relaxation of surface tensions allowed the brain to transmit the psychic energy that lay beneath the threshold of the individual's conscious self. Henceforth she would always consider herself only as an instrument of that force, which she sometimes described as "Mind" and at other times simply called "I-Mary."

With renewed determination, she devoted herself to capturing the awesome beauty of the Inyo country in poetry and prose. For her the land came alive with Presences and Powers unsensed or ignored by the casual observer. In it she found the communion with ultimate reality that she had first encountered as a child, an awareness of essential Being that both illuminated and transcended all creation. Struggling to express what she perceived, she increasingly felt the need for help with the technical aspects of her craft. Finally she decided to seek assistance from Charles Lummis, editor of the Los Angeles-based magazine, *The Land of Sunshine.*

A year spent in that city, with Lummis as her mentor, not only honed her literary talents but served to introduce her to a group of prominent people whose friendship would later prove invaluable to her career. Most important among them was Frederick Webb Hodge, the noted anthropologist and specialist in Indian ethnology, who appreciated Mary's expertise on the customs of the Paiutes. Toward the end of her stay, she sold a story to *The Atlantic Monthly*, as well as several short pieces to other periodicals. Then, with reluctance, she returned to the Owens Valley, where Wallace was now registrar of the Desert Land Office at Independence. It was discouraging to sever her connection with the circle of exciting personalities who frequented Lummis's home. But she settled into a small brown house at the foot of Kearsarge Peak, and before long her love of the land once again took over her mind.

Renewing the practices that had nourished the aloneness of her early years, she spent hours on the desert trails. Patiently she observed the life of plants and animals, recording her impressions with the precision of a scientist and the empathy of a poet. She made the desert her laboratory, looking at its myriad forms with a concentration and a reverence that transformed the looking into a celebration of seeing. And when the wells of her perception were overflowing, she began to write — *The Land of Little Rain*, a paean to the beloved country that was part of her bone and tissue.

The essays were eloquently wrought, the words chosen with exquisite care and arranged in a rhythmic style evocative of a place and a way of life that were timeless. Some of the essays harkened back to her experiences in the Tejon country; others were taken from sojourns in "the streets of the mountains," hiking the High Sierra trails. All reflected the generous passion she felt for the land, as well as her keen understanding of the people who inhabited it. In 1903 the book was published, illustrated with charming line drawings by E. Boyd Smith. It received excellent reviews and is still considered to be her best work.

Three more books followed in as many years: *The Basket Woman*, a collection of Indian tales for children; *Isidro*, a novel of early California set in the heyday of Monterey; and *The Flock*, an intimate appreciation of what she had learned about the ways of sheep and the men who tended them. In the meanwhile her marriage, from its start a source of disappointment and frustration, had fallen apart, and the burden of a mentally afflicted daughter had become intolerable. When money from the sale of her books made it possible, Mary placed Ruth in a private institution and moved to Carmel.

At the time she came to live in the seaside village on the Monterey Peninsula, she had already met George Sterling, a poet of rising fame and a central figure in San Francisco's celebrated Bohemian Club. In him she found the rapport with a fellow artist for which she had always yearned. Undoubtedly, she became infatuated with him, but it is unlikely that he reciprocated her attachment. Now in her late thirties, Mary was a short, stocky woman, with a tragic brooding face to which only her fine eyes and luxuriant, long hair lent grace. Despite her mysticism, she still longed for admiration and affection, but her aggressive approach and assertive manner tended to put people off. In addition, some of the eccentricities she had acquired, such as writing in a tree house and wearing long flowing robes, made her a target of amusement among members of the Bohemian crowd.

Nevertheless, Mary blossomed in Carmel's electric atmosphere of intellectual ferment, reveling in her close association with writers like Jack London and James Hopper, as well as with Sterling. The two years she spent there were also productive. She completed a second novel, *Santa Lucia*; a play, *The Arrow Maker*; and a superb collection of stories, entitled *Lost Borders*. Then, plagued by a pain that was diagnosed as breast cancer, she abruptly decided to go to Italy to die.

In Europe, Mary was not only miraculously cured of her illness, but she enjoyed contacts with such celebrities as H. G. Wells, Joseph Conrad, and the young Mr. and Mrs. Herbert Hoover. She returned to the United States in 1910 possessing a new confidence and sophistication. The self-assured, commanding personality that characterized the mature Mary Austin had begun to emerge. Driven by an ever-increasing need for material success and public acclaim, she established residence in New York City, where for almost fifteen years she struggled to carve out a literary career. Except for brief sojourns in Carmel, however, she was cut off from the principal source of her genius, her relationship with the earth. Though she wrote a number of books that were well received, only in the volume of essays entitled *California: The Land of the Sun* was she able to express her love for her homeland.

During her initial years in New York, Mary became involved with a group of feminist socialists and took an active part in both the women's liberation and suffragist movements. She was also briefly engaged to Lincoln Steffens, who greatly admired her unique talent for capturing what he termed "life and the poetry of life." The affair ended unhappily when Steffens lost interest, but it was through him that she met Mabel Dodge (later Luhan), who became her closest woman friend. Meanwhile, the periods Mary spent in Carmel were welcome respites from the city environment, in which she was never completely at ease.

In the tranquil seacoast community, she renewed her relationship with Sterling, for whom she still harbored a special warmth, built a house, and produced two of her plays at the Forest Theater. But more important than any other happening at that time was a fateful meeting with the man who would introduce her to the luminous landscape of Arizona and the Southwest. Daniel Trembly MacDougal was a distinguished scientist associated with the Carnegie Institution of Washington's Department of Botanical Research. He was head of both its Coastal Laboratory in Carmel and Desert Laboratory in Tucson. Mary's long-standing interest in his subject field brought them into immediate rapport. A friendship quickly flowered, resulting in frequent visits by MacDougal to New York and almost daily correspondence, in which Mary revealed her most intimate thoughts and feelings. Then, in 1919, under MacDougal's aegis, she experienced her first encounter with the Arizona desert.

On a trip with him through the Papagueria country, she discovered a wealth of fresh material for her writing. With a great surge of excitement, she realized the potential for a quality of work she had not hoped ever to achieve again. Before her month's visit was over, she had resolved to write a series of sketches, similar to *The Land of Little Rain*, which she would call *The Land of Journeys' Ending*. MacDougal agreed to collaborate, promising unlimited assistance with the research.

The book became a labor of love, which she described to MacDougal as "a monument to our common delight in the Southwest." She admonished him to keep careful notes on any information she might need. And she assured him that what she aspired to experience in his country would be "immensely more radiant and splendid" than what she had known in California. Despite a dazzling summer's sojourn in London, hobnobbing with celebrities like George Bernard Shaw, followed by a triumphant testimonial dinner given in her honor in New York, *The Land of Journeys' Ending* remained the pivotal point in her life.

In the spring of 1923 she undertook a 2500-mile motor trip through Arizona and New Mexico to gather firsthand material for the book. Ina and Gerald Cassidy, friends who were residents of Santa Fe, accompanied her and provided transportation. MacDougal was their guide on the Arizona portion of the journey, taking them on a three-day pilgrimage that included Casa Grande as well as the Papagueria. Next on Mary's itinerary were the Indian pueblo of Zuni, in New Mexico, and a visit to Inscription Rock. There Mary made the arduous climb to the top of the massive sandstone bluff, named El Morro by the early Spaniards. Later she would give a lyrical interpretation of her experience in the chapter entitled "*Paso Por Aqui*." Identifying with the spirit of this veritable island in time, she longed to remain forever at one with it. Here, she prophesied, she would always haunt.

"... You, of a hundred years from now, if when you visit the Rock, you see the cupped silken wings of the argemone burst and float apart when there is no wind; or if, when all around is still, a sudden stir in the short-leaved pines, or fresh eagle feathers blown upon the shrine, that will be I, making known in such fashion as I may the land's undying quality."*

The last lap of the journey took Mary to Ácoma, the spectacular redrock mesa on which stood the ancient pueblo known as Sky City. She climbed to the summit, assisted by two Indian youths who called her "little mother" because they knew of her zealous endeavors on behalf of the Pueblo tribes. Upon her return to Santa Fe, she collapsed from exhaustion compounded by a bacterial infection she had contracted on the trip. Taking refuge in the home of Mabel Dodge Luhan, who was then residing in Taos, Mary devoted what energies she could muster to working on the book. Ill health continued to harass her, but a tour of the Grand Canyon still had to be undertaken. By the time she left for New York, in November, she was in serious physical condition. But the grandeur of the country to which she had given herself so generously left an enduring impression.

Four years earlier, in 1919, Santa Fe had been Mary's headquarters while she was working with the School of American Research. Now, before departing for the East, she purchased a small piece of property in the town, resolving that someday soon she would return to make it her permanent home. There she would find a sanctuary, away from the tensions that characterized life in New York City.

The Land of Journeys' Ending, published in 1924, took its place as a masterpiece on a par with *The Land of Little Rain.* Some authorities consider it to be the book that best epitomizes the essence of the Southwest. As a synthesis of history, anthropology, mythology, and religion, along with detailed information on the region's flora and fauna, it surely has no equal. But the sinewy, poetic prose does more than provide factual material. Mary Austin's view of the land is holistic, a transcendent celebration of nature in its balance and beauty.

Early in 1925, Mary made the move that brought her home to her heartland. On the Camino del Monte Sol, a quiet street in Santa Fe with a splendid

* Austin, *The Land of Journeys' Ending,* p. 231.

11

outlook to the far-flung mountains, she built *Casa Querida*, her "beloved house." Focus of a budding artists' colony, the Camino had exactly the kind of atmosphere for which Mary had hoped. Her nearest neighbors were Frank and Alta Applegate, warmly generous people whom she liked at once. Other residents included Fremont Ellis, Will Shuster, and William Penhallow Henderson, whose wife, Alice Corbin, Mary had known as the associate editor of *Poetry* magazine.

Mary also delighted in the town. There on the ancient plaza one encountered scions of old Spanish families, Indians brilliantly attired in blankets, and writers, artists, and scholars as well. Best of all, commercialism was almost nonexistent. The singular quality of life in Santa Fe was a sense of rootage and wholeness that gave assurance of unity in all things. This Mary found very precious.

Before long she was deeply involved in the community's cultural affairs. First she gave support to the newly incorporated Indian Arts Fund, founded by a group concerned that the arts of the Pueblo Indians be preserved and encouraged. Prime movers in the organization were Kenneth Chapman of the Museum of New Mexico, Harry Mera, a medical doctor with a professional knowledge of anthropology, and Frank Applegate. An expert ceramist, Applegate was an authority on Indian pottery as well as other aspects of the native culture. Soon he and Mary joined forces to launch a movement that would revitalize the whole spectrum of Spanish-colonial arts. The program thus initiated bore results that far outlasted both their lifetimes. Moreover, Mary made the Indian Arts Fund the beneficiary of the bulk of her estate.

Meanwhile, she was instrumental in bringing a young photographer of Promethean talent to the Southwest. In the spring of 1927, Albert Bender, a San Francisco patron of the arts with whom Mary had been corresponding, decided that "the greatest writer in the West" should collaborate with "the greatest photographer" of his acquaintance. Accordingly, he took the then twenty-five-year-old Ansel Adams to Santa Fe and introduced him to Mary, suggesting that they produce a book. *Taos Pueblo* was the result, published three years later. In addition, Adams embarked on a project to photograph the best of the extant

Spanish-colonial arts for a book that would have text by Austin and Applegate. Unfortunately, the volume did not materialize because of Applegate's untimely death in 1931. But for Mary, Bender's visit resulted in more than books.

Their friendship blossomed into a very special relationship that brought her much comfort and joy. Albeit their contacts were mostly confined to correspondence, Bender gave her an unquestioning admiration and affection such as she had not known with any other person. Showering her with gifts, even providing material support during a lengthy siege of illness, he loved her for what she was and never found her lacking. To him she wrote, "I don't know just how you have managed it, to have me so happy to accept from you presents I refused from everybody else all my life."

During the last nine years of Mary's life, despite persistent ill health, she completed seven books, including her autobiography, *Earth Horizon*, and the novel *Starry Adventure*, in which she wrote stunning descriptive passages about New Mexico. She also found time and strength for a continuous round of stimulating activities and associations. Besides her relationship with Bender, she enjoyed close friendships with Mabel and Tony Luhan, the poet Witter Bynner, and many other interesting personalities in the area. Furthermore, there was a perpetual flow of visiting celebrities who called to pay homage to the reigning literary queen of Santa Fe. In large measure, she had achieved the success to which she had devoted a lifelong struggle. But in the end, she found her greatest happiness in being once again at one with the land.

On August 13, 1934, at *Casa Querida*, Mary Austin died quietly in her sleep following the last of a series of heart attacks. Among the rough, granite boulders at the summit of Mount Picacho, on the edge of the Sangre de Cristo Mountains, her ashes are sealed in the crevice of a rocky cairn. There she rests in eternal union with the earth, while her words live on to make known the undying quality of her country.

AUGUSTA FINK

OWENS VALLEY

THIS IS THE SENSE OF THE DESERT HILLS, that there is room enough and time enough. Trees grow to consummate domes; every plant has its perfect work. . . . Live long enough with an Indian, and he or the wild things will show you a use for everything that grows in these borders. . . .

The manner of the country makes the usage of life there, and the land will not be lived except in its own fashion.[1]

This is the nature of that country. There are hills, rounded, blunt, burned, squeezed up out of chaos, chrome and vermilion painted, aspiring to the snow-line. Between the hills lie high level-looking plains full of intolerable sun glare, or narrow valleys drowned in a blue haze. The hill surface is streaked with ash drift and black, unweathered lava flows. After rains water accumulates in the hollows of small closed valleys, and, evaporating, leaves hard dry levels of pure desertness that get the local name of dry lakes. . . .

Here you find the hot sink of Death Valley, or high rolling districts where the air has always a tang of frost. Here are the long heavy winds and breathless calms on the tilted mesas where dust devils dance, whirling up into a wide, pale sky. Here you have no rain when all the earth cries for it, or quick downpours called cloud-bursts for violence. A land of lost rivers, with little in it to love; yet a land that once visited must be come back to inevitably. If it were not so there would be little told of it.[2]

17

Out West, the west of the mesas and the unpatented hills, there is more sky than any place in the world. It does not sit flatly on the rim of earth, but begins somewhere out in the space in which the earth is poised, hollows more, and is full of clean winey winds. There are some odors, too, that get into the blood. There is the spring smell of sage that is the warning that sap is beginning to work in a soil that looks to have none of the juices of life in it; it is the sort of smell that sets one thinking what a long furrow the plough would turn up here, the sort of smell that is the beginning of new leafage, is best at the plant's best, and leaves a pungent trail where wild cattle crop. There is the smell of sage at sundown, burning sage from the campoodies and sheep camps, that travels on the thin blue wraiths of smoke; the kind of smell that gets into the hair and garments, is not much liked except upon long acquaintance, and every Paiute and shepherd smells of it indubitably. There is the palpable smell of the bitter dust that comes up from the alkali flats at the end of the dry seasons, and the smell of rain from the wide-mouthed cañons. And last the smell of the salt grass country, which is the beginning of other things that are the end of the mesa trail.[3]

Beyond that portion of the great California sheepwalk which is every man's, the desert-fenced portion between Mojave and Sherwin Hill, lies a big, wild country full of laughing waters, with pines marching up alongside them. . . . All the cliffs of that country have fresh edges, and the light that cuts between them from the westering sun lies yellowly along the sod. All the winds of its open places smell of sage, and all its young rivers are swift. They begin thin and crystalline from under the forty-foot drifts, grow thick and brown in the hot leaps of early summer, run clear with full throaty laughter in midseason, froth and cloud to quick, far-off rains, fall off to low and golden-mottled rills before the first of the snows. By their changes the herder camped a hundred miles from his summer pastures knows what goes forward in them.[4]

All streets of the mountains lead to the citadel; steep or slow they go up to the core of the hills. Any trail that goes otherwise must dip and cross, sidle and take chances. Rifts of the hills open into each other, and the high meadows are often wide enough to be called valleys by courtesy; but one keeps this distinction in mind, — valleys are the sunken places of the earth, cañons are scored out by the glacier ploughs of God.[5]

Every cañon commends itself for some particular pleasantness; this for pines, another for trout, one for pure bleak beauty of granite buttresses, one for its far-flung irised falls; and as I say, though some are easier going, leads each to the cloud shouldering citadel. First, near the cañon mouth you get the low-heading full-branched, one-leaf pines. That is the sort of tree to know at sight, for the globose, resin-dripping cones have palatable, nourishing kernels, the main harvest of the Paiutes. That perhaps accounts for their growing accommodatingly below the limit of deep snows, grouped sombrely on the valley-ward slopes. The real procession of the pines begins in the rifts with the long-leafed *Pinus Jeffreyi*, sighing its soul away upon the wind. And it ought not to sigh in such good company. Here begins the manzanita, adjusting its tortuous stiff stems to the sharp waste of boulders, its pale olive leaves twisting edgewise to the sleek, ruddy, chestnut stems; begins also the meadowsweet, burnished laurel, and the million unregarded trumpets of the coral-red pentstemon. Wild life is likely to be busiest about the lower pine borders. One looks in hollow trees and hiving rocks for wild honey. The drone of bees, the chatter of jays, the hurry and stir of squirrels, is incessant; the air is odorous and hot. The roar of the stream fills up the morning and evening intervals, and at night the deer feed in the buckthorn thickets. It is worth watching the year round. . . .[6]

Sitting islanded on some gray peak above the encompassing wood, the soul is lifted up to sing the Iliad of the pines. They have no voice but the wind, and no sound of them rises up to the high places. But the waters . . . that go down the steep and stony ways, the outlets of ice-bordered pools, the young rivers swaying with the force of their running, they sing and shout and trumpet at the falls, and the noise of it far outreaches the forest spires. You see from these conning towers how they call and find each other in the slender gorges; how they fumble in the meadows, needing the sheer nearing walls to give them countenance and show the way; and how the pine woods are made glad by them.[7]

Who shall say what another will find most to his liking in the streets of the mountains. As for me, once set above the country of the silver firs, I must go on until I find white columbine. Around the amphitheatres of the lake regions and above them to the limit of perennial drifts they gather flock-wise in splintered rock wastes. The crowds of them, the airy spread of sepals, the pale purity of the petal spurs, the quivering swing of bloom, obsesses the sense. One must learn to spare a little of the pang of inexpressible beauty, not to spend all one's purse in one shop. There is always another year, and another.[8]

. . . you may reach my country and find or not find, as it lieth in you, much that is set down here. . . . The earth is no wanton to give up all her best to every comer, but keeps a sweet separate intimacy for each. But if you do not find it all as I write, think me not less dependable nor yourself less clever.

. . . the real heart and core of the country are not to be come at in a month's vacation. One must summer and winter with the land and wait its occasions. Pine woods that take two and three seasons to the ripening of cones, roots that lie by in the sand seven years awaiting a growing rain, firs that grow fifty years before flowering, — these do not scrape acquaintance. But if ever you come beyond the borders as far as the town that lies in a hill dimple at the foot of Kearsarge . . . you shall have such news of the land, of its trails and what is astir in them, as one lover of it can give to another.[9]

MARY AUSTIN

1. Mary Austin, *The Land of Little Rain* (Boston: Houghton Mifflin and Company, 1903), pp. 87–88.
2. Ibid., pp. 3–6.
3. Ibid., pp. 158–160.
4. Mary Austin, *The Flock* (Boston: Houghton Mifflin and Company, 1906), pp. 91–92.
5. Austin, *The Land of Little Rain*, p. 183.
6. Ibid., pp. 187–189.
7. Ibid., pp. 191–192.
8. Ibid., pp. 194–195.
9. Ibid., pp. viii–xi.

21

22

23

24

27

28

29

30

31

32

33

34

35

MONTEREY PENINSULA

W<small>E STRUGGLE</small> so to achieve a little brief moment of beauty, but every hour at Monterey it is given away.[1]

. . . the lovely curve of the bay, disappearing far to the north under a violet mist, is pure Greek in its power to affect the imagination. Its blueness is the color that lies upon the Gulf of Dreams. The ivory rim of the dunes, the shadowed blue of the terraces, set on a sudden all the tides of recollection back on Salonica, Lepanto, the hill of Athens. You are reconciled for a moment to the chance of history which whelmed the colorful days of the Spanish Occupation. They could never have lived up to it.

But once on the Carmel side of the peninsula, regret comes back very poignantly. The bay is a miniature of the other, intensified, the connoisseur's collection; blue like the eye of a peacock's feather, fewer dunes, but whiter, a more delicate tracery on them of the beach verbena, hills of softer contours, tawny, rippled like the coat of a great cat sleeping in the sun. Carmel Valley breaks upon the bay by way of the river which chokes and bars, runs dry in summer, or carries the yellow of its sands miles out in winter, a winding track across the purple inlet. It is a little valley and devious, reaching far inland. Above its source the peaks of Santa Lucia stand up, having for their southern bulwark Palo Corona. Willows, sycamores, alders, wild honeysuckle, and great heaps of blackberry vines hedge the path of its waters.[2]

The modern Carmel is a place of resort for painter and poet folk; beauty is cheap there; it may be had in superlative quality for the mere labor of looking out of the window. It is the absolute setting for Romance. No shipping ever puts in at the singing beaches. Six-mule freighting teams from the Sur with their bells ajangle go by the country road. Great dreams have visited the inhabitants thereof. Spring visits it also with yellow violets all up the wooded hills, and great fountain sprays of sea-blue ceanothus. Summer reddens the berries of the manzanita and mellows the poppy-blazoned slopes to tawny saffron. Strong tides arrive unheralded from some far-off deep-sea disturbance and shake the beaches. Suddenly, on the quietest days, some flying squadron of the deep breaks high over Lobos and neighs in her narrow caverns. Blown foam, whipped all across the Pacific, is cast up like weed along the sand and skims the wave marks with a winged motion. After the equinoctial winds, whole flocks of these foam birds may be seen scudding toward the rock corners of Mission Point. Other tides, the sea slips far out on new-made, level reaches and leaves the wet sand shining after the sun goes down, like the rosy inside pearl of the abalones.[3]

The coast road, after it leaves Point Lobos behind, goes south and south, between high trackless hills and the lineless Pacific floor. From Point Lobos you can see it rise over bare, sea-breasting hills, and disappear in narrow cañons down which immeasurable redwoods follow the white-footed creeks almost to the surf. Dim, violet-tinted islands rise offshore to break the sea's assault. Now and then one ventures upon that road as far as Arbolado, to return prophesying. But the most of us are wiser, understanding that the best service the road can render us is to remain a dramatic and unlimned possibility.[4]

MARY AUSTIN

1. Mary Austin, *The Lands of the Sun* (Boston: Houghton Mifflin Company, 1927), p. 74.
2. Ibid., pp. 89–90.
3. Ibid., pp. 92–93.
4. Ibid., p. 97.

41

42

43

44

45

46

47

48

49

50

51

THE SOUTHWEST

BㅤETWEEN TUCSON AND PHOENIX, south of the paved road, there
is a vast cactus garden that I can never pass without crossing my fingers against
its spell. Often in the midst of other employments I am seized with such a fierce
backward motion of my mind toward it as must have beset Thoreau for his
Walden when he had left it for the town. So that if I should disappear some day
unaccountably from my accustomed places, leaving no trace, you might find me
there in some such state as you read of in monkish tales, when one walked in
the woods for an hour and found that centuries had passed. Look for me beyond
the last spur of Santa Catalina, where there is a one-armed sahuaro having a
hawk's nest in the crotch. Beyond that there is a plantation of thistle poppies
on the tops of whose dusty green stems have perched whole flocks of white,
wind-ruffled doves, always about to take flight and yet never freed. Then small
droves of *Opuntia Bigelovii*, like lambs feeding with their tails between their
legs; here and there a bisnaga, dial pointed above its moving shadows; silvery
flocks of cholla, now and then a sahuaro pushing aside the acacia under which
its youth survived, or a stiff, purple-flowered ironwood, and droves and droves
of cholla leading down to the dry arroyo, from which at intervals arise green
cages full of golden palo-verde flowers.[1]

Here, where I write, on the lower slopes of Sangre de Cristo, as the hills
go toward the *plan del Rio*, when the bridle-rein is slacked, your horse brings

you, by traces discovered only by the feel of the earth under his foot, to unfenced fields that, except for the wavering furrow of the plow across them, are still of the Small-house period. Here the surface run-off of the August showers is still led down to the great corn plant by dikes and ditches, from the open ends of natural catchment basins; childishly simple to the eye and cunning with the experience of three thousand years.

There is something inexpressibly stirring thus to happen, where all around is silence and the sun, on plants that have come down this long way with man, as though they gave off something of man's personality, absorbed through centuries of aspiration with him, up from the grass. The soul of the corn passes into the soul of the observer; the insistent beat of consciousness soothes to a murmur, faint as the wind in the corn, of godhead in man, to which the Small-house People, giving ear, were moved like the corn in the wind. It is only in such passages that one realizes that the charm of Amerind life, for the modern American, is the absence of those strains and resistances that stiffen us against the wind forever blowing from some quarter of the universe across our souls.[2]

It goes on still and forever, this silent working together of man and the grass of the field. . . . Go heedfully where you go, then, along the trail borders. Break no bough needlessly, and uproot no seeming weed. Who knows which of them awaits on the tardy opportunity which your indifference delays, of inestimable cooperation?[3]

I doubt if any white man ever completely knows an Indian. . . . All that I propose to show you is something of the rainbow-shine of the pueblo bubble, fouled by our handling, but unbroken. Even then I shall probably not be able to show it to you without at the same time dimming it with my own breath.

The root whose substance makes all the bubbling shapes, is Life, conceived as a reality, forever flowing and reforming through all phenomena. At the bottom of the Amerind mind, this reality is probably seldom personalized. Anthropologists, who have agreed to speak of this universal element by the word describing it among certain of the plains tribes, *wokonda*, agree that there is less of manness in the names it goes by in the terraced towns . . . than goes to our own notion of a Supreme Being. Certainly it is never thought of as being weary, jealous, complacent, or avenging. This *wokonda* is, in some degree, in every created thing, stick and stone, bird and beast and blowing wind. It flows endlessly from shape to shape; the great bison is a majestic form of its tarrying, the sun a place where *wokonda* is concentrated, the corn one of the blessed disguises which it takes on in order that men may be fed. There is a pueblo myth of how Life assumed the deer, from which it is released by the huntsman's arrow, to take on fresh shapes for his following.

"O younger brother," said Cushing's Zuni host to him, concerning the water turtle, "it *cannot* die; it can but change its house."[4]

. . . there is never a season, in the cañon of the Rio Grande, without its appropriate, its inevitable color scheme. In the snowy months there will be cumulus clouds topping the cañon walls, white as cotton bolls, burnt-orange tips of the willows repeating the note of the cliffs, and bright flecks of bluebirds' wings, interlacing earth and sky. When the snowdrifts in the shadows begin to take lilac tones, the drift of wild plums is feather white, the rabbit-brush white fluff over green, and the water shadows as green as the junipers. In September the wild plums are vermilion, with a bloom like the purple haze of the mountains, and after the plums the Virginia creeper tones with the frost-bitten red of the cliffs. Then the squashes piled in the fields, and the bright gold of the rabbit-brush bring out the yellow of the clays, and the adobe huts which otherwise tend to disappear into the earth from which they have been drawn, are blots of flaming scarlet and vermilion. In Española Valley where *chile* is raised for export, not only the house walls, but great racks of threaded pods make splashes of heartening color, clear and detached, color that gives you a full sense of its being eaten and absorbed. About this time the cottonwoods along the acequia madre begin to bear, in place of leaves, little heart-shaped fruits of light. . . . Along Tesuque River they come up burning like the bush in the midst of which was God. Toward the end of October the deep, self-contained blues, the delicate fawn, and the grape-black shadows of the winter landscape emerge.[5]

There is an effect of mountains on man as fear. I recall once, of a summer night, climbing the steep cumbre of one of the Rio Grande potreros, terrified to find the moon almost at my shoulder, a near and menacing object, mistress of hollow space from which, so lightly poised it was, I might by ill-considered movement displace it dangerously. I should not, I know, if I lived in that country, move about much at night without first performing all known acts of propitiation.

But neither do men go to places they fear, if they can help it. Yet all about the Tewa world the high places where nobody need go except for such business, on Lake Peak, on the crest of Oku, sacred Tewa turtle, and on the high peak of Jemez there are shrines, centers of deep trails of many many moccasins. Also I find this strange, that the places where the most shrines are known to be, such as the potreros between Cochiti and Shufine, west of the Rio Grande, and the Small-house country on the upper Chama, are the places in which people who know neither the shrines nor the country find themselves walking with the prick of expectancy between their shoulders, with the stirring of some familiar unfamiliar sense. . . .

What we felt there, may well be the residue of personality that man leaves in all places once frequented. What presences, then, have been among the mountain-tops to raise in us the response that is called holy! For to the aboriginal, to be holy is to be filled with strange, abundant life.[6]

The moment comes and goes. Not beauty only, for there is a special kind of beauty for every hour the mountain knows, beauty which man perceives without participating, beauty to which he feels himself a stranger. There is the beauty of the structureless gloom of gathering storms, beauty with terror of the milling maelstroms of the air, beauty edged with intolerable loneliness of the moon-bow flung on the fluffy, silver-flecked floor of cloud observed from peaks above the tree line. There is beauty of the mountain meadows, to which the response is a joyous sense of well-being, lakes like jade, jeweled with water-lilies, long bajadas thick with the plumes of bear-grass bowing like white ladies to the royal wind. From all these we come back, knowing that long before men set up an anthropomorphic deity there was a state, easily met among the mountains, called holy, being whole with the experienceable universe.[7]

MARY AUSTIN

1. Mary Austin, *The Land of Journeys' Ending* (New York: The Century Company, 1924), pp. 129–130.
2. ibid., pp. 72–73.
3. Ibid., p. 283.
4. Ibid., pp. 246–247.
5. Ibid., pp. 177–178.
6. Ibid., pp. 383–385.
7. Ibid., pp. 389–390.

61

63

64

65

66

68

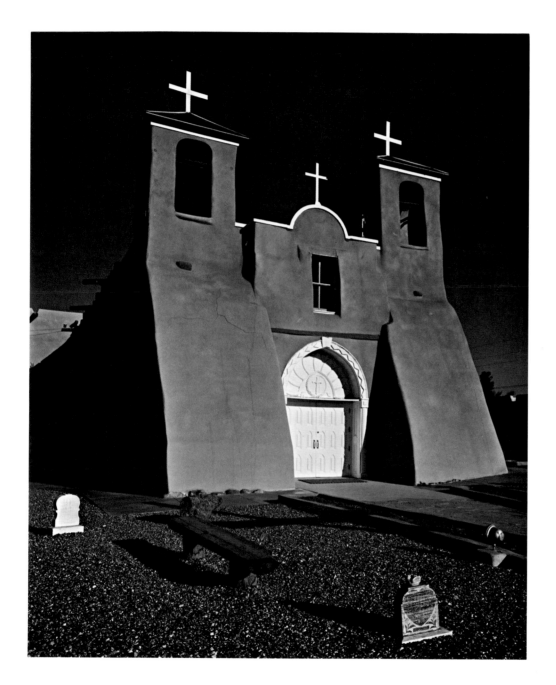

69

70

72

73

74

THE PHOTOGRAPHS

DESIGNED BY NANCY SOLOMON
COMPOSED IN LINOTYPE ALDUS
WITH WEISS DISPLAY TYPE
PRINTED ON QUINTESSENCE DULL
AT THE PRESS IN THE PINES

NORTHLAND PRESS

BOUND BY ROSWELL BOOKBINDING
PHOENIX